THE SECOND NIGHT OF THE SPIRIT

OF THE SPIRIT

Bhisham Bherwani

THE SECOND NIGHT
OF THE SPIRIT
Bhisham Bherwani

CavanKerry ◈ Press LTD.

Library of Congress Cataloging-in-Publication Data
Bherwani, Bhisham
The second night of the spirit / Bhisham Bherwani. – 1st ed.
p. cm.
ISBN-13: 978-1-933880-11-2
ISBN-10: 1-933880-11-2
1. Brothers–Poetry. 2. Loss (Psychology)–Poetry. 3. Family–Poetry. I. Title.

PS3602.H47S43 2009
811'.6–dc22

2008050636

Cover art, Winslow Homer, *Moonlight, Wood Island Night*, 1894
The Metropolitan Museum of Art, Gift of George A. Hearn, in memory of
Arthur Hoppock Hearn, 1911 (11.116.2)
Photograph © 1980 The Metropolitan Museum of Art
Author photograph by Martin Desht
Cover and book design by Peter Cusack

First Edition 2009
Printed in the United States of America

CavanKerry Press Ltd.
Fort Lee, New Jersey
www.cavankerrypress.org

NEW ◈ VOICES

CavanKerry Press is dedicated to springboarding the careers of previously unpublished poets by bringing to print two to three New Voices annually. Manuscripts are selected from open submission; CavanKerry Press does not conduct competitions.

CavanKerry Press is grateful for the
support it receives from the
New Jersey State Council on the Arts.

ACKNOWLEDGEMENTS

This book would not have materialized without the cooperation and support of my family and without encouragement and guidance from Chard DeNiord, Adil Jussawalla, Joan Larkin, Anne Marie Macari, Marie Ponsot, F. D. Reeve, and Michael Waters.

I would like to thank the team at CavanKerry Press, especially Joan Cusack Handler, Peter Cusack, Florenz Eisman, and Baron Wormser, for its meticulous attention to every detail in the making of this book.

"The Second Night of the Spirit" was published in *The Dirty Goat.*

To my mother, my brother,
and the memory of my father

CONTENTS

FOREWORD BY CHARD DENIORD   xi

THE RETURN OF THE PRODIGAL SON   2

I

AUTUMN   5
DIAGNOSIS   6
LESION   8
CANT / DESCANT   10
CATHARSIS   12
LOOMING   15

II

THE SECOND NIGHT OF THE SPIRIT   19

III

HEMLOCK AND HELLEBORE   34

FOREWORD

Bhisham Bherwani declares in his poem "Hemlock and Hellebore," an elegy for his father, that he is "a scryer scrying the void" through glass and water. Indeed he is. Accepting the formidable challenge of translating his compound grief over his brother's severe mental handicap and his father's death in 2000 into evocative poetry, Bherwani succeeds courageously in transforming the details of his brother's illness and father's passing into powerful keening. His strategy for turning the private facts of malady and loss into universal language lies in his fine-tuned admixture of objective description and heart-rending lament. With one eye on the hard facts of his brother's encephalitis and the other on the emotional trauma of witnessing the disease's ravages, Bherwani chronicles his remorse, his grief and his journey as a poet, with, to use Philip Larkin's profoundly mimetic phrase from his poem "Talking in Bed," "a unique distance from isolation." Bherwani depicts this "isolation" with spare, lyrical strength in his description of his old passport photograph, an image that prompts this confession of his "madness" as a symptom of his guilt over escaping the same fate as his brother.

> A passport
> the size of my hand sits on my shelf,
> inside it a photo, shot an instant
> I don't remember ...
> ... My brother and I sit
> cross-legged. The print's edges must be frayed,
> like the passport's, or wrinkled like its pages
> stamped in black or blue or red, visas
> to places where I want to travel light.
> *Wanderlust!* You say; but neither
> wandering nor lusting, but something else,
> a failure to escape, keeps me moving.

Madness! you propose, to which I say,
yes, though maybe you could think up
another word.

The irony of Bherwani's "unique distance" from this childhood picture lies in his simultaneous closeness to it. This distance is unique for its doubleness, both the remoteness and intimacy it affords in his terrible need "to travel light," to escape that which he is only compelled in his obsession to keep coming back to, namely his "special" brother and his parents in Bombay. Bherwani sustains the motif of travel as a paradoxical trope for his emotional stasis—his "unique distance from [his] isolation"—throughout the book. In elegizing his father in the last long poem, he admits to his ghost-like existence as a grief-stricken wanderer in New York after his father's death of a blood disease in Bombay. Even the monuments and memorials that comprise his sought-after new home in New York appear to him in his grievous fugue state as mere generic constructs.

I am lost between domes and steeples,
rotundas and parapets, stone porticos
engraved with names, titles, and elegant
credentials: *Statesman and Scholar,*
Benefactor and Trustee, … I walk past them.

Like a hierophant, Bherwani leads his reader from the intractable, disease-ridden world in which he lives, what James Wright called "this scurvy and disastrous place" in his poem "To the Muse," to his interior world of pathos and poetic urgency. As a witness and brother, he achieves a keenly disinterested view of himself as a solitary yet universally familiar son. By invoking such mythological figures as Orpheus, Demeter, Persephone, Aesculapius, Phoebus, Thalia and Melpomene, he adds diachronic weight to his "scrying." Although he risks mere erudition at the expense of poetry in making so many mythological references, Bherwani employs his allusions in the service of elegizing, weaving Greek muses, gods and demigods into his poems as integral imaginative characters in the saga of what "hurt him into poetry." I especially admire Bherwani's invocation of Aesculapius in his title poem, "The Second Night of the Spirit." In this extended metaphor, which is also a persona poem (as the italics indicate), Aesculapius performs figurative neurosurgery on the brother.

Anesthetized I lie across the bed feeling
nothing; Aesculapius standing

behind, raising caduceus—

tip sterilized in pure asphodel
petal extract, sharp as a sword blade—

jabs at it, his healing stick, through my forehead

into skull. …

… As with a toothpick, he picks from the lobe
a morsel

out of its calcified cage

and sets it on a table.

Having successfully repaired the brain, Aesculapius then offers it to Bherwani as a sacred anodyne. Doubling as both physician and priest, Aesculapius echoes Love's offering of Dante's "burning heart" to Beatrice for consumption in the first sonnet of La Vita Nuova.

… Aesculapius,

holding out the throbbing brain to my brother,

wakes him and says:

"Eat."

And, albeit reluctantly, my good brother
eats, while Aesculapius blesses him and weeps.

The elements of love, originality, imagination, allusion, verbal economy and figurative inspiration come together here in a private myth that moves the reader with universal force. This poem reads as a testimony to love's genius in the context of extremity. Bherwani's variation on love's visceral archetype of agapaic cannibalism boldly expresses the transcendent power of the transpersonal self.

The uniqueness of his specific distance lies in Bherwani's self-abnegating perspicacity. He is, in his view on his rightful place in his family and society, a victim of a very cruel fate that has ravaged his brother and left him, the "lucky" sibling, as a healthy but helpless witness of nature's caprices. Poetry thus serves as Bherwani's consolation, his only means of transcendence from his inescapable, although unfounded sense of culpability. But his cathartic sympathy, as well as imagined empathy, stops short of redemption with only "a sliver of light like hope." Such self-indicting scrutiny allows him in turn to testify powerfully to the lurid procedures and tasks love gladly endures in its care for another, transforming something as unpleasant as an anal procedure into a moving act of agape.

> … papa pins him face-
> down on the bed, his pajamas lowered, buttocks
> exposed while mummy withdraws from his
> rectum her finger, dipped in mustard oil,
> little white worms squirming along its length.

In his pilgrimage to find some peace, Bherwani feels "condemned to seek out the elusive / edifice for the taciturn, nameless survivor," knowing that he will "fail, finding at best / an anonymous gazebo overlooking a pond, lake, / river, sea, or ocean." This nameless outpost from which Bherwani examines his life provides his only sanctuary. In his failure to find a "survivor"—himself and his brother restored—in the "elusive edifice," he goes on trying nonetheless with the determination of T. S. Eliot's speaker in "East Coker" "to recover what has been lost / and found and lost again and again." Also like Eliot's speaker, he knows that "home is where one starts from." In the terrain between home and his gazebo, Bherwani writes on the move, but it's as if he is still and the world is moving around him, so fixed is he on his love for his brother. As Bherwani's reader, I feel like a privileged guest in his anonymous gazebo. It is a deeply moving place to be, a real place as well as an internal stage on which a powerful family drama is played out in originally conceived, highly personal poems that make universal connections. Bherwani has filtered his sorrow through the alembic of both his heart and mind in *The Second Night of the Spirit*, eliminating in the process his griefs for that potent concentrate of distilled grief. The slightest taste of it is overpowering. Such a feat is truly remarkable in any book, especially one's first.

—Chard deNiord

THE SECOND NIGHT
OF THE SPIRIT
Bhisham Bherwani

Before the beginning of years
       There came to the making of man
Time, with a gift of tears;
       Grief, with a glass that ran;
Pleasure, with pain for leaven;
       Summer, with flowers that fell;
Remembrance fallen from heaven,
       And madness risen from hell; . . .

              (Swinburne)

THE RETURN OF THE PRODIGAL SON

I am the prodigal son
returning, father, not because your hired
servants have bread enough to spare, because I do not
perish in hunger, and have fattened on meat,
caviar, and wine. I return to renounce these.
I return to renounce frivolous
journeys to countries remote and strange,
debauchery my affable guide,
so debonair, so charismatic,
and though sometimes unrelenting,
sometimes savage, always
loyal.
      I have disowned him.
His influence, father, is widespread.
He hounded me city to city,
street through street, but I would no longer be
swine.
      I felt something.
Was it your far-flung blessing I felt?
Or did I exhaust my part of it,
gorging and whoring?
My brother's part has deservedly multiplied.
He has been your faithful son. His brain
damaged by disease, he has been your light
and I your darkness. Father, I have
betrayed my brother, his mind
troubled. Will he forgive me?
My riotous living has been without peace.
Will you take me as one of your hired

servants, father? I am unworthy to be called
your son. I will become my brother's
keeper, I will administer him
medicine.

                Will he forgive me then, father?

Brother,
       will you forgive me,
please,
brother?

I

AUTUMN

Essex County, New York, 2006

My friend, his toddler son, aged three, and I,
along an Adirondack backwoods trail,
watch how the leaves have turned. Beyond a veil
of mist, autumn's fiery cornucopia
radiates above a brook.
                         On a whim,
the boy lets go his father's hand to skip
alone across the leaf-strewn, wooden bridge.
"It's getting dark," his father cautions him.
I think of my brother aged three, little,
nauseous with encephalitis, in pain
entering an endless night as febrile
illness permanently damages his brain.
Almost forty years have since gone by.
I'm through with nature's inveterate cycles.

DIAGNOSIS

Encephalitis is the inflammation of the brain. Arthropod-borne virus-
es, invisible to our naked eye, can cause it. A bite by a "carrier"
(or "vector") bug can be fatal, especially if the victim's immune sys-
tem is already weakened by disease, like cancer or HIV, or if he's
old or very young.

A child bitten, say, at the age of two might be
unable to say what he's feeling, what's
happening. Possible symptoms are severe headaches,
nausea (with vomiting),
confusion,
                          disorientation, memory loss,
hallucinations,
drowsiness, convulsions, problems
communicating, and more, a change, for instance,
in personality, though that might follow the blurring
of senses and the slurring of speech, until
any semblance of speech is only imagined, only
wished-for. Such debilitating fevers can be
symptoms of severe and irreversible
brain disorder.

                          Have you watched a child with such
an affliction? He might, without blossoming, grow
handsome: 6'2", eyes thoughtful, lashes
long, lips full, brow high,
and a nose not *only* his mother considers aristocratic;
grow through phases of pubic hair forming, of voice deepening—
deepening enough so that the garbled words that rise
as screams are not the screams of a frustrated

child or adolescent, but of an adult, less shrill;
deeper;
        deep enough for me to hear them when I am
away, far, shuttling between cities.
I am grateful for them.
              The dark patches that will
surround his eyes in time from years of pounding
head against furniture, fists against temples,
from years of medication, will not make him, my brother,
less handsome to me; and not less noble.

LESION

Electroencephalograph,

I don't understand you: I'm awed
by your map of troughs and peaks

of this dance of 10,000 million neurons, a half-hour synopsis

for a boy of ten who stopped by
thirty years ago.
                    You're telling me—

this much I can fathom—he should've been in school,

fifth grade, instead. He never went to the fourth,
third, second, first, or kindergarten. So

relentless you are—how the patterns zigzag to the page's

edge.
          What follows beyond the right margin?
What precedes the left?

The boy's my elder brother, his last

epileptic fit on record two weeks before
papa died.

Where did this dance begin? Where is it going?

If you went on, no doubt you would again turn

downward.

               Would you stop?

I'll follow you (I want to know what goes on there).

I'll dance to the beat of the dance you map
in perfect step.

O Sibyl,

you're quiet,
so noncommittal.

Am I not good enough to dance on the Stygian banks?

Electroencephalograph,
I'd like to shred you to bits.

CANT / DESCANT

He's been taken to doctors and he's been taken to priests,
and he's been studied by all breeds of physicians and prophets.

They've promised this and promised that but haven't promised a cure. Still,
there's always a follow-up appointment to keep.

"Bring the boy back next week."

Shall I admire their relentlessness and optimism?

"Bring the boy back next week."

Why?

What is he? *A guinea pig?*

Fuck you.

Fuck you and fuck the sham shamans who blame it on the devil.
Fuck them, and fuck the devil: I will in my rage
possess him and fuck him.
And forget not the quacks in their white aprons, fucking con artists.
Fuck their reams of empirical data and their clinical observations.
Fuck their med school degrees, their bank accounts, and their investments.
Fuck charts.
                    Fuck prescriptions and drugs, fuck reports of medical
breakthroughs.
Fuck MRIs. Fuck X-rays.
And the psychiatrists and the psychologists:

fuck their fancy analysis, because
none of this drivel lights up my brother's eyes
like his mother's kiss.

CATHARSIS

I remember a Kodacolor print—
of my brother and me sitting on the grass—
hanging above a sideboard somewhere,
in an aunt's house, maybe, or somewhere else; maybe
I have not, after all, really seen it.
But I remember it—if something not seen
can be remembered—as I recall
mad July monsoons softening the earth
soiling our nylon shorts, as in the photo.
The abundance for some is a nuisance, so much
overflow clogging streets. I smell damp
tropical earth whenever I remember
the photo, walking along Riverside Drive,
through Azabu Juban's gardens,
in the shadows of Cologne's Cathedral or
Rome's Coliseum; I carry it,
wherever I go, like a passport.

                                        A passport
the size of my hand sits on my shelf,
inside it a photo, shot an instant
I don't remember, forgotten like most instants.
Or maybe this *is* remembering,
remembering the Kodacolor is forgetting.
The print is old, if three decades,
give or take a little, is old,
if childhood is young. My brother and I sit
cross-legged. The print's edges must be frayed,
like the passport's, or wrinkled like its pages
stamped in black or blue or red, visas

to places where I want to travel light.
Wanderlust! you say; but neither
wandering nor lusting, but something else,
a failure to escape, keeps me moving.
Madness! you propose, to which I say,
yes, though maybe you could think up
another word? There are words for everything, even
for the many kinds of madness. But call me
mad, humor my plainness, let's not argue.
I don't argue with the specialist when
he calls my brother mad—
for my plainness, so that I understand.
The monsoon has been mad, overflowing
filth from excess rain flooding Bombay's streets,
Colaba to Sewree, roads along which
a school-bus takes my brother with forty other
crazies—if you can't think to call them
something else—to a school, so "special,"
made just for them. Who knows the meaning of *special*
and is able also to explain it?
Walk with me.
                    I'm tired of walking alone.
I will show you a photo in which I'm
smiling, Thalia and Melpomene
fighting over me, a catfight in the sky,
Thalia, winning, nowhere in sight.
Maybe I *can* remember what I have
not seen, after all, know such things, somewhat,
things like madness.
                    There is madness
in the monsoon. My brother is weaving
cloth on a handloom in an ill-lit room

beneath rain pattering hard on the roof
at the school for special education.
The bus will bring him home. I'm turning around
from the end of some promenade.
Melpomene is now winning, this one
instant extrapolated like a photo.
What's a photo if not
the catharsis of an instant on glossy background—
forms, my brother's, mine, our brows alike,
apprehended by one lens, one eye—floating
invisible for a while in some fluid,
and emerging into view, as from a womb,
under the dim lamp of a darkroom?

LOOMING

From one end to the other, a yarn
runs back-and-forth across a wooden handloom,
cotton warp and weft threads
symmetrically crossing.
I turn
its creaking handle clockwise, sitting in an ill-lit room.

One moment faster, slower another,
I weave
morning through afternoon, half a turn of loom handle
on average each second.
I weave till the bell rings and we gather
in the schoolyard, board our buses, and leave.

Below are the playground and the driveway;
around, tenements and slums;
behind, a crumbling building, visible
through a dirty windowpane. The room's dusty,
gloomy even; on a bright day,
when sunlight comes,

rays blur, tumbling over dust particles.
Fingernails cram with dirt in minutes; like a membrane
dust settles on everything, on dangling spider webs in the corners,
on the spiders. It's rained hard since last night;
everywhere outside are wet grit and puddles.
In a way, though, this place is a haven.

The spider must do something—something

useful—spin,
                  from filaments, a web;
that is its purpose, what god would have it do
inexorably; irrevocably, its destiny.
For reasons to me a mystery, I'm spinning,
year after year into cloth, countless miles of thread.

Streaks of sunlight—unexpected—
flash through the downpour, projecting
skewed shadows across the room; twenty machines
in motion dance across floor and walls, as many heads and pairs of arms
monotonously moving; overhead,
the monsoon is hysterically pattering.

The sunshine could be Persephone
smiling, still in Hades,
anticipating her visit to Demeter.
I hope she'll stay. It'll then be bright forever.
My loom could be a lyre, and I could be
the one who'll coax her here, Orpheus.

I,
Orpheus, am damned to looming
above Persephone's world
below. I understand her world's horrors,
the sorrows of hell's inhabitants. I
understand also horrors of this world in which I'm spinning.

I dream I play my friends a song on a lyre.
Retarded, autistic, cerebral palsied—they dance to its air;
along Acheron's banks, they seek a shortcut to
Elysium's center. They speak unspeakable

miseries; in their eyes terror,
they dance one behind the other in despair.

Love connects us like our chronic labor
miraculously binds yards of yarn into cloth; threads interleave
creating fabric, crisscrossing, as things in nature must—
day and night, wakefulness and sleep,
refuge and fear—
offsetting ordeals through which we feel and breathe.

From one end to the other, a yarn
runs back-and-forth across the wooden handloom,
cotton warp and weft threads
symmetrically crossing.
I turn
its creaking handle clockwise, sitting in an ill-lit room.

II

The first night or purgation is bitter and terrible to the sense. The second transcends all description, because it is exceeding fearsome for the spirit, as we shall presently show . . .

(St. John of the Cross)

THE SECOND NIGHT OF THE SPIRIT

For my loins are filled with a loathsome disease: and there is no
soundness in my flesh.

(Psalms)

I

The sea extends past the fishermen's ferries, hemp nets
stretched against undercurrents like auguries;
extends

past floating silhouettes calibrating
the horizon. Silvery clouds from there to here
were flooded for an instant with fading shades of amethyst.

*

Silence is the playground
swing's amplitude
diminishing—

creaks and rasps of chains and levers—

waning—

monkey bars a molecular structure, the sapphire sky its backdrop.

*

Dusk, the windsurfing
waif,

tacks this way over the swelling evening waves.

*

Silence is the dinner table being
cleared,
                    clamor of silverware in
the kitchen sink,
my mother's ring clinking
on porcelain,
steel, and aluminum,
water

gushing over her soapy fingers,

my father sipping his whiskey, smoking a cigarette.

*

Night, the windsurfing
daemon,

tacks ahead.

*

I retire to my bedroom, facing east, to study. Across the hall,

*

my brother retires to his bedroom, facing the sea.

Pigeons loiter on the concrete parapet jutting
beneath his windows, grunting, wings
fluttering at the wind's
whip flinging

faster, and farther

and farther,

hooting

in.

*

Who is it? Who

*

comes in from nowhere?

*

Silence is waves lapping the shore
breaking

wildly, brine-scent ascending through the mist.

*

O cœlum! O terra!

*

This side of the wind a mantis clasps a window-
pane in my brother's room,
shivering.

*

Flashes, fast in succession, show my brother's
features, Adonis-like, dark, lips
innocent, hand, palm

up, relaxed on forehead; then, above the wind:
thunder, pigeons' wings flapping,

brine-smell; mantis gone.

*

O heaven! O earth! What an enemy is this?

*

We must not struggle with God.

II

What thought?
                Or is it thought that enters my brother's
mind when early into the night his brow

furrows? What thought when his gentle eyes look
afraid and confused, lost in the vision of some

inexplicable dread inside? When he clenches his fist,
what does he think?

Or is he only feeling, not
thinking? He raises his fist—

not a full fist, more like fingers
clenched tightly and held up in revolt,

momentarily, in the sea-mirrored moonlight
—and,

wrist bent, slaps his head
hard at the temples so it is heard,

strident and unmistakable, in neighboring rooms—
resounding

whack—flesh-and-bone striking
flesh-and-bone. Does something (someone?) inside him

feel it? Why does my beautiful brother repeat it
until the night begins to echo

*thud*s? He screams
suddenly, his eyes streaming

tears. Why is his cry
so guttural

and sad? He strikes forehead with fist and pounds
head against furniture

and wall,
sobbing and screaming. O God, *stop—please—*

shattering yet another night with head-blow
drumbeats and earsplitting cries. Stop

battering the boy. Our mother trembles
praying, standing

beside her powerless, maddened son who takes her hands,
folded in prayer, and bites them—

cutting clean crescent to bone through
bleeding flesh. Her blemishes

set in night after night, etching
into her once-pristine delicate flesh like birthmarks.

She drapes her sari's
fringe over hands at wedding parties,

the same hands that now hold out
for her son a glass of water and medicine.

Our father, brazen
in the face of this ineffable

wrath, proffers
body for blows,

bites, and scratches, his arms,
hands, and face

scarred, fresh
wounds red and

bleeding, older ones, white
arcs, impressing

into flesh. How close father and son become wrestling
their common enemy.

*

It avails not to promise Craterus gold mines for a cure.

*

It ceases.
                    In fits and starts, it
stops. My brother's cheeks wet from incessant

crying, face bruised, self-
inflictions blackening;
                            but for the occasional

slap to head or slam
against wall,

it ceases. He sobs and gasps. Senses
regained, fatigue overcomes him.

Exhausted, baffled by
the outcome of his and not his

doing, he surveys the room, with eyes
saddening, like a conqueror, the aftermath

of his rage, and he is overwhelmed
with remorse.
                              My brother

reaches to embrace mother and father.
The moon moves east to west

lighting the sea's receding tide; our mother
brings from her dressing table a bottle and cotton swabs.

The room fills with the bittersweet
smell of calendula ointment to heal the scars.

*

In this night of the spirit there is
a guilty one.

He escapes, unscathed: next morning he goes to school,
face and hands unscarred, uniform impeccably pressed

creaseless and starched by his mother.
In this night of the spirit, there is

a guilty one.

III

Healer of healers, Aesculapius,
visits one night; holding out a cup, he says,

"drink." I drink the wine, its jasmine bouquet

pleasing. He beams and fills the cup again and says,
"drink," and I drink another cup of fermented asphodel.

And he refills the cup once more to the brim and I

drink, again and again until he says
we're ready:

"Now."

Anesthetized I lie across the bed feeling
nothing; Aesculapius, standing

behind, raising caduceus—

tip sterilized in pure asphodel
petal extract, sharp as a sword blade—

jabs it, his healing stick, through my forehead

into skull.
The wound is clean.

He pulls out the stake, rinsing

bloody apex in a bowl of asphodel nectar.
Then, as before, raising

caduceus, he stabs precisely through the fresh

hemorrhage,
widening the gash,

turning stick this way and that against

obstinate bone,
deepening it so spearhead touches

brain—

deep enough to tease the frontal lobe—
through arterial pools to where some million neurons

cluster, closely huddled at the source of all

sensation. As with a toothpick, he picks from the lobe
a morsel

out of its calcified cage

and sets it on a table. Religiously he repeats this
act—picking through cranium each time a different

morsel, placing it, nerve and tissue,

on the table, precisely—relative to the soft
cumulative mass—not unlike a three-dimensional jigsaw

puzzle,

until the lobe lies outside of me completely
reconstructed.

His work not finished, he repeats from the beginning:

goring this time my temples to reach the parietal
lobe, and reassemble it, piece by piece,

with the temporal, outside

my body. Through a stab in my nape
he draws the occipital lobe

unwaveringly out

until on the table lies within his reach,
in its entirety, my brain.

He scoops it into his palm and holds it

up in the moonlight, marveling at his handi-
work and its architecture,

one shadowy terrestrial system in miniature

held up against another
as fathomless. He blows on the brain; it begins

pulsing.

I sit up, winded,
heart beating fast.

He blows on the brain; it pulses

faster. Each time
he blows on it it pulses

faster still. When he stops, its pulsing

time and rate is that of my heart's
beating, rhythm of brain and heart synchronized

perfectly. Aesculapius,

holding out the throbbing brain to my brother,
wakes him, and says:

"Eat."

And, albeit reluctantly, my good brother
eats, while Aesculapius blesses him and weeps.

III

O thou whose only book has been the light
Of supreme darkness which thou feddest on
Night after night, when Phoebus was away;
To thee the Spring shall be a triple morn.

(Keats)

HEMLOCK AND HELLEBORE

Kishin Mulraj Bherwani (1937–2000)

> We are poor passing facts,
> warned by that to give
> each figure in the photograph
> his living name.

1

Panacea's gait must be like my mother's
limp the way I remember it one afternoon in
March 2000 entering the dining room,
jetlagged; a spontaneous smile
commensurate with the surprise of this
unannounced visit home—my impromptu
intercontinental trip—welcomed me as she hobbled
over to kiss me, to bless me. Sunlight gleamed
through the windows facing east, everything
sparkling, the marble on the floor, the glass tabletop,
the silverware she clutched in her hand.
Nowadays, she smiles more reticently,
reluctantly even, troubled by the thrombo-
phlebitis, calves sheaths of chronic pain as she makes
her way from room to kitchen, kitchen to
bazaar, bazaar to office; she is stubborn, she won't stop
driving, my imploring is useless; negotiating
Bombay's traffic is for her a sleight of hand
on steering wheel. I watch a distended foot
shift from brake to accelerator as red becomes

green on Colaba Causeway's busy stretch where,
finding at the intersection no traffic
policeman, my mother makes a long
prohibited right at Electric House, telling me
it should be, as it once was,
permissible. I watch a hand, soft
and veined, settle again on the recoiling
wheel, bracing myself for the impending
homilies: everything I do, everything I don't,
distresses her. I am condemned to this. My way-
wardness and wanderlust, my divorce,
my disregard for what she regards
conventional, my cavalierism trouble her.
Obstinacy she can overlook, maybe
forgive even—it runs for me in *both*
sides of family—but the rest will lead me
where?

*

     I walked into the office, carry-on
over shoulder, straight from the airport. My father,
speaking on the phone, beamed. He moved
thick folios from a chair to make me room.
We drank tea. He opened a Chippendale
cabinet, mirrored inside, reflecting
bottles of scotch, vodka, and rum, cigarillo
tins, matchboxes, ashtrays, and stationery
strewn about. He needed a pen. He limped,
stepping cautiously, deliberately. Granite,
leather, wood: this was a man's place.
The Arabian Sea, sprawling beyond its shores,

glared in sunlight through the windows.
I was a nobody in a New York corporation,
squandering spring afternoons of my life's
best years in cubicles beside pantries or photo-
copiers, between corner offices with lesser
nobodies in slicker suits and silkier ties
who bragged after hours in midtown bars
about which still lesser nobody to wheedle
next en route to the thickly carpeted
offices upstairs. Papa started with a
pittance of a bank loan—for his paltry
collateral, another loan—and single-handedly
built his merchant trading firm:
you'd know from his hands'
hardness, his discipline and punctuality;
you'd know from the awe the staff regarded
him with, papa sauntering down the hall,
even, those last few numbered years, with a limp.
There was pain behind the uncontainable
smiles, I sensed it, the plainest of pains,
surpassing all possible pains—physical pain—
sharp and sure, definitive pain. Lethal
pain. He would not admit it. His smiles
were numbered. I hadn't seen him
in two years. In two months he'd be gone
forever.

*

There is in a limp a kind of resolute
nobility exaggerating the corporeal,
masking the indestructible, eternal

41

spirit within some arcane, dark
chamber with the only secrets that matter.
I am condemned, sitting with pen and paper—
wherever I sit, in Bombay, in New York,
somewhere in between—to the inescapable
failure of narrating the incommunicable,
to trying, like a grafter to shatter invisible
locks to others' impenetrable chambers.
I scribble one futile line after
another, each at best another doodle.
I am cursed. If I had a limp I'd have
inside me a chamber to tap. Meanwhile,
I scrawl like an outsider to suffering,
documenting the staggering steps of the chosen
crippled while I await my own inevitable
demolition.

*

My brother's limp is the most
enigmatic. He's too stubborn to subject himself
to medical tests, too strong for any good
doctor to pin down alone. It is not chronic,
something physically straining at school
might trigger it once every few months.
It exhausts him; he lies down,
pampered with meals in bed and eucalyptus-
based liniment applications. The smell
fills the apartment as he walks from room
to room following mummy. First, it was
papa, but suddenly papa who was there was not
there; less than one week in the hospital, then

a corpse laid out on the living room
floor for the rites, flesh cold and heavy.
I had to dress him.
Seven men propped up the body.
I'd called him *wounded*
lion

        in the ambulance; he had that kind of
gait the last time he left the office, ever. His senses
faded his first night in the dialysis room, his
penultimate night. He did not know
where he was. He mumbled, speech
slurred, words barely decipherable, "I'm afraid,"
he said. "I'm afraid of living with *torturous*
pain." Raging leucocytes—multiplying—
warring four years with erythrocytes and intravenous
chemotherapy cycles were winning, each cycle
tendering false hopes, "drawing me out,"
he said. During treatments he kept
beside him business accounts, studying the thick
folios, updating them, numbers endorsing a life-
time of back-breaking hard work: overstuffed
suitcases lugged from airport to airport,
through foreign cities. Before the fatal
complications

        he had me play him Tchaikovsky
—*Swan Lake*—on the Walkman. Before
the final, one-way, ambulance ride, lying
in bed at home, he quoted me
Pope—"A little Learning ..."
—when I suggested he ought to
treat his condition as if ...

        "Drink deep, ..."

He was in experts' hands—

                      "or taste not …"

—but their interminable
optimism, to the mortal moment, couldn't
coax fate. I look out a window onto
Harlem's 125th Street. It is March 2006.
The night plays out like a film.
I am in New York. I am in Bombay. Beyond
the pane is my reflection; beyond
the reflection are cars; beyond the cars
the wounded lion, merciless
god's puppet, bellows with barely enough
breath to roar between
deafening gasps, pleading—no,
not pleading—ordering—not ordering, no—
daring

          the young doctor to dismantle, once
and for all, the life-support system, the one
way out of his one—*torturous*
pain—trepidation. How much had he
endured already that the limp hid? I want to reach out
past the street, past the cars,
buildings, trees, and lampposts, past
their retreating shadows at dusk, and say
papa.

       Papa?

           They wheeled him—shouting,
wheezing—out from Dialysis to Emergency
upstairs. But he wasn't made for such
confinement, such dark, constricting spaces.
He must have wanted to be laid out, even if

for an hour only, in *his own* living room
in Bombay's munificent early May sunlight,
surrounded by family and relatives,
associates and friends. We brought my brother
out from his bedroom into the mayhem.
He folded his hands in prayer for the soul of
his father, his best friend. Of all
horrors, the plainest horror—the horror of
the void, the *annulled*—is the most
pitiless. The two were inseparable.
I read my brother's medical reports:

... he was normal till the age of two years
and ten months. He had a bout of hyperprexia ...
his father was away for six weeks. He was
very much attached ...

                  They walked together, half-
limped sometimes, on the promenade downstairs
along the coast each evening: my brother
and this motionless mass on a makeshift stretcher
I would carry with three other men
into a hearse to have it
compacted by an electric cremator
to a handful of ashes in a clay urn.

2

Mummy's smile is enigmatic. It's a ruse,
I suspect, like a limp, sidetracking me from what
I'm after. What horrors has *she* internalized?

The reports bear more than just her impalpable
fingerprints, sleepless nights, and blood-
stains. I stare at the pages, as if they were some
subversive artist's grotesque
creations. I am condemned to seek out
the elusive impulse for his conceptions. I am condemned
to fail. Papa's mother doted on her first
grandson.

He was normal till the age of two years ...
He lost his grandmother around the same age
and his father was away for six weeks. He was
very much attached to both ...

      Does a void get smaller, as dubious
conventional wisdom has it, with time, with days
evaporating like seawater in the tropical sun
to be forever sluiced away by monsoon
downpours? Does it steadily
contract, so that it all but
vanishes into an oblivion beyond mind's
grasp, leaving behind a trace of its presence that
erupts only in recurring dreams? What if *time,*
itself, compresses, pushing
present back into past, thrusting
past toward present into one
instant as undying as it is fleeting
under the force of its own uncontrollable
velocity: March 1966, January 1969, March
2000,
      May 2000, March 2006?
Does the void, then, under pressure,

conflagrate, uncontrollably
expanding to enclose that infernal wretch
—night—to absorb it completely and, with it,
you?

*

Mummy's king-sized bed is half vacant.
My brother gravitates to the master bedroom.
He always has, but there is about it something
conspicuous now, something pre-Newtonian—
more fundamental, more mysterious,
than mechanics, more rudimentary than
calculus—an undetectable magnet betraying its
inestimable ethereal force. Mummy weeps more
in the monsoons, staring into the rain and over-
cast sky through windows shut to keep them from
swinging uncontrollably in cyclonic
winds and slamming. Her tears are always
stifled, her lamentation is never clean, never
a burst like a torrent. Always gasps, always
bird-like fluttering. I want her to stop.
I plead her.
                    She doesn't stop.
I scream at her.
She doesn't stop. I slam doors, I curse
the weather. She doesn't stop. I curse
god. She is inconsolable. She is
a girl. Her moist cheeks, shining, are soft. Angelic,
she is a seraphim gazing out as if that is where
her void is, as if that's where it's always been.
My brother stretches out where papa slept.

He extends his arm toward her
and grunts. There is no sense in anything.
I am beset by the brutality of nonsense.
My brother sits up and walks to the bathroom.
He brings out a towel. He stands beside her,
looming above her frame, pressing
towel to her face, dabbing her cheeks. I watch
void offset void
like negatives that must
negate each other into an elemental
emptiness so dark that from it can emerge
nothing but a sliver of light like hope.

He was very much attached …
A change in his behavior was noticed.
He was very restless and lacked sleep.

I am calm. I cajole her. We are a molecule—
she is its nucleus—atoms of a complex
organic structure situated each at our intricate
angles, none independent of the others,
bound forever by imperceptible
tugs, vibrating unremittingly within our god-
given amplitudes at our respective loci,
never at rest.
                    He used to lie down beside
papa, wedging himself conveniently between
mother and father, beaming at being their
center of attention. He beams now
when he has her undivided attention, and mine.
He makes us smile. He makes us laugh.
I am surrounded by books in New York,

48

in Bombay. They are useless, they make me
brood. I am condemned to brooding: *useless
books*. They are to me what my brother's
blanket is to him, the blanket he carries
everywhere, covering himself on bed,
on sofa, even during dog days, even in mid-
May's heartless heat. Some shrink has a theory
about my brother and his blanket. Smart
shrink. He must have a theory
about me and my books. The wind,
sweeping his face, my brother
sits by the window displacing the sunlight,
shifting it, refracting it, even, like a
prism, scattering it—heightening its
brilliance, as I watch him eat, to something
unreachable, the evanescent
pitch of an aria: not a soprano,
no, something higher, something in its delicacy
beyond understanding. He is a diamond.
Not a diamond, no, something else, something more
of a dodecahedron, Platonic matter for
constellations, the heavens—for things
cosmic—rays reflecting
off stained white pajamas, stained
white sleeveless undershirt, dispersing
off his decaying teeth, smile each day more
toothless. He changes the sunlight. He makes it
sad. Chocolates are his sweet
curse, Japanese his favorite, then Belgian, then
Italian and Swiss, in that order. His smile is his mother's
soft spot. He will manipulate her with a smile
and an outstretched arm, grabbing her wrist,

tugging her while she limps behind cursing—
glutton!—after dinner to the fridge
stocked with chocolate, his other hand clutching
blanket,

        flung over shoulder, dragging across the
floor.

*

        I am a scryer scrying the void
through the early spring air. I am trying
to enter it through atmosphere, the emptiness
on the other side of the pane
mummy gazed into after tearing into bits
papa's love letters. I look out a window onto
Harlem's 125th Street. I will scry the void
through glass. My mother is on the pane's
other side. It is raining, a seasonal downpour surrendering
remnants of a winter chill still in the air.
I am wearing papa's navy pinstripe suit.
It has a few more years of wear, good weave,
English wool. Or I am in the white Levi's
I wore to the crematory, frayed at cuffs,
torn at crotch. I am an atom suddenly gone
astray within its molecular bounds.
I call my mother.
We talk.
        She insists I am
hesitant; she insists there is something
I want to tell her, something
I'm keeping from her. I insist there is
nothing. My books are worn at their

spines. I want to cover them. I want to re-
organize them, alphabetically by author.
Or title.
I want to polish my shoes.
I want to vacuum the carpet.
I want to get my hair cut short, to a crew.
Or shorter.
We hang up.
I look out the window.
My mother is on the pane's
other side. It is raining. I am an atom
inexplicably realigned within its molecule.
Panacea's voice must be like my mother's.
Her father was a homeopath, disbursing gratis
measured drops of concentrated
flower extracts, deadly
in excess, but in an expert's
temperate hands magically potent
cures. He doted on his first, his only, daughter.
The daughters of healers must suffer: it is written
in some ancient book; I must find it. I look
out the window. My mother smiles, holding out
two cups to her sons: one has a hemlock potion;
the other, a hellebore.

3

I am lost in buildings' shadows. Like papa,
I take to cities. I take their streets in
my stride: fifty blocks, a hundred blocks, a hundred-
and-fifty blocks. I am in Bombay, I am in Brooklyn,

in Amsterdam, in Osaka. I retrace his steps,
sometimes inadvertently. I gravitate to the water.
If not ocean, I'll settle for sea;
even a riverbank with a promenade
bristling in the sun will do. I walk past shanties
along the holy Pushkar lake, bordering
the Rajasthan desert. The water is warm,
dazzling. I scatter papa's ashes
and enter a tenement beside a temple.
The heat outside is July's,
brutal. Inside, it is cool, the priest
returning from an alcove
carrying a book bound of parchment,
one of thousands in the archives, not one
catalogued. There is a tradition that is
a mystery: it will belie and defeat all logic,
all mathematics; it will dispense a musty parchment
on demand from a last name, one out of thousands,
tens of thousands, of last names.
A gecko will scuttle out from between
pages and scurry across the dusty, clay floor.
I watch papa's name scrawled after papa's
papa's name. He was a magistrate. His voice, great-
uncles will tell me, was deep: courtrooms
shook when he spoke. He had no enemies:
he was fair. The ashes are dispersing
in the lake. I am a scryer scrying the void
through water. If not lake,
I'll settle for pond. Even a puddle
between mossy rocks will do, *especially* a puddle
between mossy rocks. The geese are flying
north above the Hudson. There is a mossy patch

off Riverside Park, cradled between
wet rocks, barely a puddle, but still
teeming with something like life. My hand goes in
completely, to wrist, and deeper, sunlight's
refractive ploy. I look inside: there is not one
hand; there are two: one is my brother's.
The sun is cold. The sun is cruel.
We are in Bombay. I am five. He is seven.
We are in nylon shorts and polyester shirts,
squatting on rocks above our favorite
puddle in Breach Candy, the sea ten meters away,
roaring. Our hands are little. The fish are
little, thin, and fast in the puddle, their swimming
more like wriggling. We will never
catch any. Their swimming is more like a
writhing, like papa on his last night twenty-
five years later, or like my brother five years later,
screaming as papa pins him face-
down on the bed, his pajamas lowered, buttocks
exposed while mummy withdraws from his
rectum her finger, dipped in mustard oil,
little, white worms squirming along its length.
Chocolates are his curse. He will be denied them
until he tempers his habit, until he is
rid of virile worms that love
sweets more than him. The sun is setting
across the Hudson, over the New Jersey shore.
It has shrunk my hand. I pull it out.
I look at it. It is teeming with something like life.
The cherry blossom stems in Sakura Park
are stirring. It is March 2000.
Papa is in his office. I have an inter-

continental flight confirmed. I call him.
I am devious: what would he like from New York
if, *hypothetically*, I were to visit, say,
in two months? *Nothing*, he says, *you: I'd like
you.* But I insist. *Bring me a flower*, he says.
I am not devious, I am wretched.
I don't bring him a flower.
I deny him *that.* Not a pressed orchid, not
even a seed. What is left to deny after denying
love? I deny him what would have been his last
cigarette two days later at the office. I
extinguish it. What good are bright marigolds
scattered over a corpse? What good is rose
water? What good is wild tobacco?

*

The sun has shrunk me to oblige
the void. It is setting on my right; the moon
is rising on my left, hovering
between Riverside Church's gothic
tower and splendid façades fading into
silhouettes. I am lost between domes and steeples,
rotundas and parapets, stone porticos
engraved with names, titles, and elegant
credentials: *Statesman and Scholar,
Benefactor and Trustee,* ... I walk past them.
I am condemned to seek out the elusive
edifice for the taciturn,
nameless survivor. I will fail, finding at best
an anonymous gazebo overlooking a pond, lake,
river, sea, or ocean. If not ocean ...

I'll settle for a puddle, *especially* a puddle
between mossy rocks, anything that cradles
a void with something in it
like life. The sky is flushed pink. I take,
like papa, to cities. They are elaborate
wombs, interiors lush with a little gaiety, a little
sadness, like a dark café where a man sits
alone beside a hearth with pen and paper
scribbling one futile line after another,
gazing now and then into the twilight through
windows beyond the candlelit tables.

Interiors

within interiors, chambers
within chambers:
like an opera house during a Donizetti
overture, or an auditorium where a string
ensemble plunges into an incessant
pizzicato, while outside shadows of Doric
pillars crisscross on the square,
beside the fountain, under a vernal moon.

NOTES

THE SECOND NIGHT OF THE SPIRIT

The Latin references—*O cœlum! O terra! Unde hostis hic?* ("O heaven! O earth! What an enemy is this?"), *non est reluctandum cum deo* ("we must not struggle with God"), and *nil uvat immensos Cratero promittere montes* ("it avails not to promise Craterus gold mines for a cure")—are from a compilation of quotes about demonic possession in Robert Burton's *The Anatomy of Melancholy*.

HEMLOCK AND HELLEBORE

The epigraph is from Robert Lowell's poem "Epilogue."